To the scientists and the photographers who share their magic worlds.
— CS

To Dad, the great adventurer who is made of the same stuff as Shackleton!
With much love. — JR

Published in English in Canada and the USA in 2022 by Groundwood Books
Text copyright © 2021, 2022 by Claire Saxby
Illustrations copyright © 2021, 2022 by Jess Racklyeft
First published by Allen & Unwin Australia in 2021

Groundwood Books / House of Anansi Press
groundwoodbooks.com

With thanks to David K. A. Barnes, marine ecologist at the British Antarctic Survey and lead author of "Icebergs, sea ice, blue carbon and Antarctic climate feedbacks" in *Philosophical Transactions of the Royal Society A: Mathematical, Physical and Engineering Science* 376, 20170176, for his expert review of the North American edition.

We gratefully acknowledge the Government of Canada for its financial support of our publishing program.

With the participation of the Government of Canada
Avec la participation du gouvernement du Canada | Canada

Library and Archives Canada Cataloguing in Publication
Title: Iceberg : a life in seasons / Claire Saxby ; Jess Racklyeft.
Names: Saxby, Claire, author. | Racklyeft, Jess, illustrator.
Description: Illustrated by Jess Racklyeft. | Previously published: Crows Nest, NSW: Allen & Unwin, 2021.
Identifiers: Canadiana (print) 20210364963 | Canadiana (ebook) 20210364971 | ISBN 9781773065854 (hardcover) | ISBN 9781773065861 (EPUB) | ISBN 9781773065878 (Kindle)
Subjects: LCSH: Icebergs—Antarctica—Juvenile literature. | LCSH: Seasons—Antarctica—Juvenile literature. | LCSH: Animals—Antarctica—Juvenile literature. | LCSH: Antarctica—Climate—Juvenile literature.
Classification: LCC GB2597 .S39 2022 | DDC j551.34/209989—dc23

The illustrations were created in watercolor, acrylic painting, collage, pencil, ink and digital illustration.
Designed by Sandra Nobes
Printed and bound in China

FSC
MIX
Paper from responsible sources
www.fsc.org
FSC® C144853

ICEBERG

A LIFE IN SEASONS

Claire Saxby   Jess Racklyeft

GROUNDWOOD BOOKS
HOUSE OF ANANSI PRESS
TORONTO / BERKELEY

In the final freeze of an Antarctic winter,
green tails wave across a star-full sky,
as if to farewell endless nights.

If this world looks empty,
look closer.
Those are penguin tracks,
and beneath the ice, orca roam.

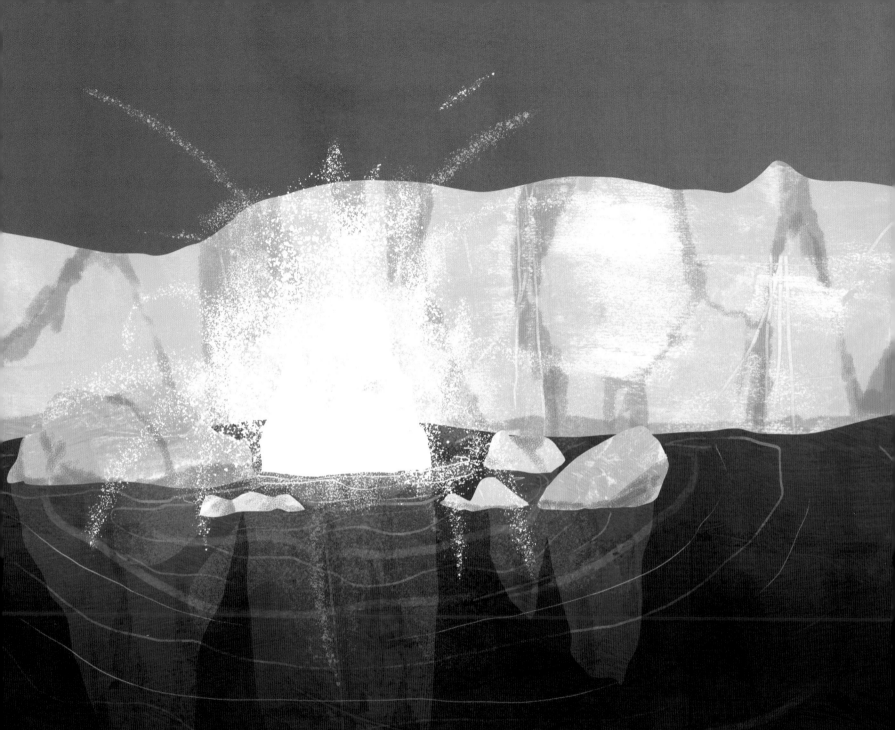

In the pale morning, an iceberg calves — shears from a glacier
and plunges to the ocean in a haze of sparkle-frost.
The iceberg is flat-topped, sharp and angular
and carries ancient weather in its layers of ice-clothing —
a coat for each year volcanoes blew
and black ash fell like snow.

If this world looks empty,
look closer.
Birds are coming.
They know about Antarctic summers.

The new iceberg bobs in the water,
an unfettered island, its mountain hidden underneath.
Waves ripple *away, away-o,* to quiver at the pack ice.
Cracks unshackle algae suspended all winter,
and under-ice krill stir.
They know summer is near.

Leopard seals lurk
as a raft of penguins explode
like black-and-white rockets from an ice hole.
Fish-fat and sleek, the emperors belly slap,
then begin the inland trek to feed hungry chicks.
Adélie parents take turns to perch
as meltwater trickles past their rock-nests.

Summer arrives. Sun sparkles on a murk-green sea.
Clouds of krill swim shallow and deep, feed and grow.
Days stretch and nights shrink
until the sun just taps at the horizon.

Humpback whales spiral,
filter krill from giant mouthfuls of sea.
Penguins dive deep for fish.
Seals dive deeper to twitch-whisker hunt.

Fish hunt salps.
Terns wheel overhead.
Blue-eyed cormorants, too,
their wingspans wider than
outstretched arms.

Squid chase krill.
Birds chase squid.
Orca gather, linger, watch and seize.
Short-tailed shearwaters feast then return
to their chicks.

The iceberg drifts where the currents push,
where the winds blow.
Summer sun softens edges.
Undersea currents wash at the hidden mountain.

Autumn brings shorter days.
The sea *cools, cools, cools.*
Visitors depart –
to the deep,
to warmer islands,
to tropical birthing waters,
to faraway summers.

Seals cluster around holes until they, too, close.
Loose frazil crystals extend and join.
Flip-edged pancakes jostle and raft.
Rafts become floes.

Sea ice thickens.
Krill retreat to underberg hollows
to wait out winter.

This iceberg – every iceberg –
is winterbound, icebound, seabound. Stuck.
Sometimes rain falls,
but mostly the sky swirls snow or
    ice crystals in this frozen desert.
Winter tides swell and ebb.
Nights fall and fade.
Storm winds rage down inland mountains,
mound long snow furrows
and only fade when they find the sea.

It may seem winter will never end
when the sun fails to breach the horizon
and even aurora trails only sometimes appear.
Just wait.

Spring returns.
Waves *lap-lap-lap* the iceberg until it looks velvet-soft.
Currents drag.
Winds push.

The iceberg twists, tilts, rocks, shears.
It is old now – tall and small and mellow.
It eddies into a sheltered bay,
tips and falls.

This world is not empty,
nor ever still.
Far from the places we know,
it feels everything we do.

Ocean, sky, snow and ice,
minute greens and giant blues
dance a delicate dance.

In another pale Antarctic dawn,
an iceberg calves,
settles to the sea.

MORE INFORMATION ABOUT OUR POLAR REGIONS

Global warming is increasing the temperatures in all our oceans, but not evenly. Seemingly small temperature rises can have a big impact, particularly in Antarctica (a continent surrounded by ocean), as well as in the Arctic (a region made up of continents and oceans).

How our planet responds to climate change is complicated. For example, melting sea ice can slow the growth of some algae, and krill populations may be similarly declining. This in turn reduces the food available for larger animals in the food chain. However, less sea ice also means more light enters the sea and so algae are around for more of the year. This provides longer meal times for algae-eating life on the seabed.

Some animals featured in this book, such as certain species of penguins, are found only in Antarctica. Others, such as short-tailed shearwaters and orca, can also be found in the Arctic, which provides a unique habitat for polar bears and narwhals. Far south and far north (literally polar opposites!), Antarctica and the Arctic are both affected by climate change, but in different ways.

These polar regions have environments like no others on earth. Finely balanced and fragile, they inspire awe, deserve understanding and need our protection.

ARCTIC

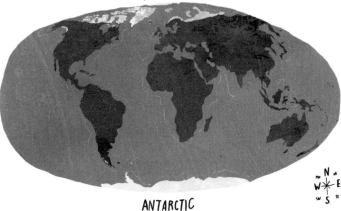

ANTARCTIC

GLOSSARY

Algae — tiny single-celled organisms, sometimes called phytoplankton, that live in water and can convert light into food through a process called photosynthesis.

Aurora — bands or sheets of green, red or yellow light that wave across the night sky. They are known as aurora australis or southern lights in the Antarctic, and as aurora borealis or northern lights in the Arctic.

Floes — pieces of floating sea ice. An ice floe may measure as little as 7 feet (2 m) in diameter but can be larger than 6 miles (10 km) across.

Frazil — fine ice crystals or plates of ice suspended in water. They are the beginnings of sea ice (when the sea surface seasonally freezes).

Glacier — a huge mass of ice that moves slowly over land, sometimes ending in the sea. Polar glaciers are often called ice sheets because they blanket the land and spread out in all directions.

Krill — very abundant ocean creatures that look like small prawns or shrimps, and provide food for whales, seals, penguins and other seabirds. Five Antarctic krill weigh about the same as a spoonful of sugar!

Meltwater — water from melting snow or ice, particularly from a glacier.

Pack ice — a mass of ice floating in the sea, formed by pieces of all sizes and ages freezing together. May include raft ice, floes and icebergs, so ships try to avoid pack ice.

Pancakes — mainly circular pieces of ice, ranging from 12 inches (30 cm) to 10 feet (3 m) across, that have raised edges from bumping against each other.

Raft ice — cakes or sheets of ice that overlap each other.

Salps — tiny jelly-like, mostly transparent sea animals, each shaped like a cylinder. They grow to about 4 inches (10 cm) and can be found in long chain-like colonies, or wheels.